SCIENTIFIC AMERICAN | EDUCATIONAL PUBLISHING

SCIENTIFIC AMERICAN INVESTIGATES FOSSILS

PETRIFIED FORESTS

BY NATALIE HUMPHREY

Published in 2025 by The Rosen Publishing Group
in association with Scientific American Educational Publishing
2544 Clinton Street, Buffalo NY 14224

Cataloging-in-Publication Data
Names: Humphrey, Natalie.
Title: Petrified forests / Natalie Humphrey.
Description: New York : Scientific American Educational Publishing, an imprint of Rosen Publishing, 2025. | Series: Scientific American investigates fossils | Includes glossary and index.
Identifiers: ISBN 9781725352049 (pbk.) | ISBN 9781725352056 (library bound) | ISBN 9781725352063 (ebook)
Subjects: LCSH: Petrified forests–Juvenile literature.
Classification: LCC QE991.H86 2025 | DDC 561'.16–dc23

Portions of this work were originally authored by Kathleen Connors and published as *Petrified Forests*. All new material in this edition is authored by Natalie Humphrey.

Designer: Andrea Davison-Bartolotta
Editor: Natalie Humphrey

Photo credits: Cover, p. 1 (main) William Cushman/Shutterstock.com; cover, p. 1 (dirt texture) komkrit Preechachanwate/Shutterstock.com; cover, p. 1 (stone texture) Efefne Design/Shutterstock.com; cover, p. 1 (vingette) Yurlick/Shutterstock.com; p. 5 Lost_in_the_Midwest/Shutterstock.com; p. 6 Sascha Burkard/Shutterstock.com; p. 7 EWY Media/Shutterstock.com; p.8 BallBall14/Shutterstock.com; p. 9 (bottom) Tracy Brucks/Shutterstock.com; p. 9 (top) robert paul van beets/Shutterstock.com; p. 10 Aaron J Seltzer/Shutterstock.com; p. 11 Cavan-Images/Shutterstock.com; p. 12 FCG/Shutterstock.com; p. 13 GEA Stock/Shutterstock.com; p. 15 (main) Bret J. Unger/Shutterstock.com; p. 15 (inset) Vasilii Aleksandrov/Shutterstock.com; p. 17 (top) Francisco Blanco/Shutterstock.com; p. 17 (bottom) Frank Romeo/Shutterstock.com; p. 19 Juan Carlos Munoz/Shutterstock.com; p. 21 SHISHIGAMI GRAPHIX/Shutterstock.com.

Some of the images in this book illustrate individuals who are models. The depictions do not imply actual situations or events.

Printed in the United States of America

CPSIA compliance information: Batch #CWSA25. For Further Information contact Rosen Publishing at 1-800-237-9932.

Find us on 

CONTENTS

Words in the glossary appear in **bold** type the first time they are used in the text.

FOSSILIZED WOOD

Fossils are the marks or remains of living things that form over thousands or millions of years. While most people think of dinosaurs or animals when they think of fossils, plants can make fossils too! **Petrified** wood is one kind of plant fossil that you can find around the world.

By looking at petrified wood and other plant fossils, scientists can put together a more complete picture of what the **prehistoric** world may have looked like.

Some petrified wood
fossils may look like
stones, but others look
like colorful trees.

HOW TO MAKE A FOSSIL

How do wood fossils form? First, a tree may be buried in **sediment**. The sediment presses down on the wood for many years, keeping it soft and close to the condition it was in when it was buried.

For most wood fossils, different types of **minerals** replace the wood, leaving a fossil behind. Some wood fossils, though, aren't completely replaced by minerals. These wood fossils may still have **organic** material left over.

In petrified wood, all the wood in a tree is replaced by minerals.

FUN FACT
FOSSILIZED WOOD CASTS FORM WHEN MINERALS FILL A MOLD, OR FORM, LEFT BY WOOD. SOME OTHER WOOD FOSSILS ARE FORESTS HIDDEN IN THE WATER!

PERMINERALIZATION IN WOOD

Petrified forests are commonly made up of wood petrified by permineralization (puhr-mih-nuh-ruhl-ih-ZAY-shun). Permineralization starts when minerals in water flow into a tree and fill spaces inside and between cells.

Petrified forests in the western United States are largely made from wood that's been replaced by the mineral silica. Millions of years ago, trees were buried in sediment created by **volcanic** ash that contained silica. When it mixed with water in the ground, the silica moved into the wood and started permineralization.

The many colors of this
petrified wood are beautiful!

SILICA

Silica can sometimes make petrified wood very colorful. Silica can become quartz, a mineral that forms crystals and changes color based on traces of other minerals in it. If the mineral chromium is present, the wood can even look green! However, some petrified wood still looks like regular logs.

Petrified forests don't look like modern forests. The trees in a petrified forest are often broken and laying on the ground.

PETRIFIED BOG WOOD

FUN FACT

CHALCEDONY, AGATE, AND OPAL ARE COMMONLY FOUND IN PETRIFIED WOOD.

DATING PETRIFIED WOOD

Petrified forests can be millions of years old, but they aren't all the same age. It depends on when the forests were buried. For example, a petrified forest in California is about 3.4 million years old, while one in Arizona is more than 211 million years old!

Scientists can figure out how old petrified forests are by studying the rock they were buried in. If the petrified forest is surrounded by a **layer** of old rock, the petrified forest is probably just as old.

Scientists can also use **radiometric dating** to figure out how old petrified wood is.

FUN FACT

WHEN SCIENTISTS LOOK AT THE AGE OF ROCKS SURROUNDING A FOSSIL TO FIGURE OUT THE AGE OF THAT FOSSIL, IT IS CALLED SUPERPOSITION.

TREE RINGS

To study trees today, scientists often look at the circles found inside a tree's trunk. These circles are called rings. If there is a lot of rain and sunlight in an area, trees grow faster, and the rings are further apart. When there is less rain or sunlight, the tree will grow slower, and the rings will be closer together.

By looking at the spacing on a tree's rings, paleobotanists can learn about the **climate** of the ancient world.

By looking at fossilized trees, scientists can tell if an area that is a desert today may have been a riverbed millions of years ago!

PETRIFIED FOREST NATIONAL PARK

One of the largest petrified forests can be found in Arizona. The wood was so beautiful, many people started to take it. However, **conservationists** wanted to keep the forests safe.

In 1906, some of the area became Petrified Forest National Monument. It became Petrified Forest National Park in 1962. This national park now covers 346 square miles (896 sq km). It is now illegal to take pieces of petrified wood out of the park.

FUN FACT

NATIVE AMERICAN PEOPLE HAVE LIVED IN THE PETRIFIED FOREST NATIONAL PARK AREA FOR THOUSANDS OF YEARS.

Over 800,000
people visit
Petrified Forest
National Park
each year.

NATIONAL
PARK
SERVICE
Department
of the Interior
PETRIFIED FOREST
NATIONAL PARK
UNITED STATES DEPARTMENT OF THE INTERIOR
NATIONAL PARK SERVICE

AN ANCIENT LOGJAM

Long ago, many trees grew along a river in Arizona. After the trees died, they floated down the river and got caught together in logjams, or backups. In time, these logjams became the different "forests" in the park.

Scientists have found nearly 14 different species, or kinds, of trees in Petrified Forest National Park. They have also found that many of the trees were huge! Some of these trees may have been around 200 feet tall (61 m) while they were alive.

While scientists know the trees in Petrified Forest National Park are different species, they don't know what kind of trees they are.

SEE IT YOURSELF!

Would you like to see petrified wood up close? While the petrified forests in Arizona and California are popular, there are many more petrified forests in the United States. The Theodore Roosevelt National Park in North Dakota has many petrified trees. Yellowstone National Park has petrified forests too!

The United States isn't the only place to find petrified forests either. In Egypt, the Maadi Petrified Forest is around 35 million years old. One of the largest petrified forests is found in Lesvos, Greece.

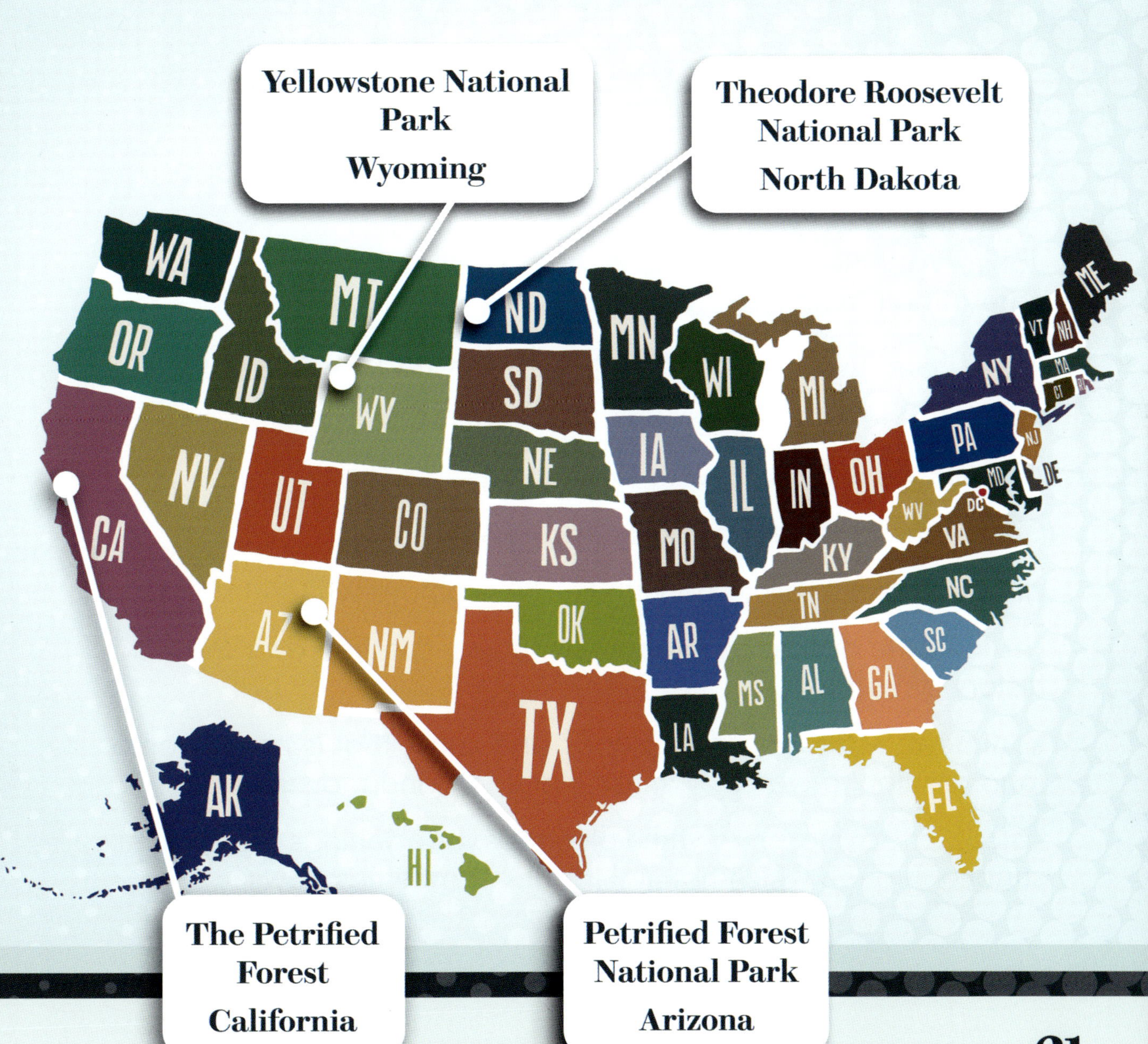

Petrified Forests In the United States
Yellowstone National Park
Wyoming
Theodore Roosevelt National Park
North Dakota
The Petrified Forest
California
Petrified Forest National Park
Arizona
WA
OR
MT
ID
WY
ND
SD
MN
WI
MI
NY
ME
VT
NH
MA
CT
NV
UT
CO
NE
IA
IL
IN
OH
PA
NJ
DE
MD
WV
DC
VA
CA
AZ
NM
KS
MO
KY
TN
NC
OK
AR
SC
TX
MS
AL
GA
LA
AK
HI
FL

GLOSSARY

climate: The average weather conditions of a place over a period of time.

conservationist: A person concerned with conservation, or the care of nature.

layer: One thickness of something lying over or under another.

mineral: Matter in the ground that forms rocks.

organic: Having to do with living things.

petrified: Something being turned to stone.

prehistoric: Having to do with the time before written history.

radiometric dating: A method of finding out time over the long history of Earth.

sediment: Matter, such as stones and sand, that is carried onto land or into the water by wind, water, or land movement.

volcanic: Having to do with volcanoes, or openings in a planet's surface through which hot, liquid rock sometimes flows.

FOR MORE INFORMATION

Books

Burgan, Michael. *Weird But True!: Rocks & Minerals.* Washington, DC: National Geographic, 2022.

Amin, Anita Nahta. *Dig and Discover Fossils.* Oxford, UK: Raintree, 2024.

Websites

National Geographic Kids: Petrified Forest
https://kids.nationalgeographic.com/nature/article/petrifiedforest
Discover more about petrified wood and how it forms.

National Park Service: Park Fun
www.nps.gov/pefo/learn/kidsyouth/parkfun.htm
Plan a visit to Petrified Forest National Park in Arizona and learn all of the fun things you can do while you're there!

INDEX